D1097820

OFFICIALLY
WITHDRAWN

RIDDLE RADDLE, FIDDLE FADDLE

Ann Bishop

Pictures: Roy Mathews

ALBERT WHITMAN & Company, Chicago

The best way to collect riddles is to ask everyone you know for help. This is exactly what I did, and I wish to thank all the people who told me and sent me their favorite riddles, especially—
Elizabeth and Deborah Swartz, Belmont, Massachusetts,
and
the children of Hedges Central Elementary School
and their school librarian, Miss Bonnie Hopf,
Mount Vernon, Indiana,
who helped me the most with enthusiasm as well as riddles.

From reading fairy tales and myths, you know that answering riddles could be a serious, not to say a dangerous, business. If a princess had many suitors, she or her father, the king, asked a riddle. The man with the right answer won the bride. Travelers were as often beset by riddles as dragons. The wrong answer caused no end of trouble. Give me a toll road any day!

If you know what riddles were asked at a certain time and place, you have clues to what people were interested in, joked about, and used in everyday living. Some old riddles are nearly impossible to guess because churns, dippers, and quill pens, for example are unknown to us. In a few years some of our funniest new riddles may be just as hard to guess.

Riddles often change to keep up with the times. The first riddle I ever heard was, "What's black and white and red all over?" I learned it was a newspaper, but maybe you think it's a blushing zebra. Only last month I heard it was a chocolate sundae with catsup!

While it's handy to have riddles collected in a book, they are really meant to be spoken aloud. A riddle is to share, not to hoard. And sometimes the answer doesn't make sense—or nonsense—until you say it aloud. This is because many riddles depend on puns and use words like *gnus* and *news* that sound alike but aren't alike in meaning or spelling.

Let me end with a riddle. What's new and often old? The answer you've guessed is right—a riddle!

ANN BISHOP

What's black and yellow, and goes
"Zzub, zzub"?

Where does a worm go in a cornfield?

Why does a spider spin a web?

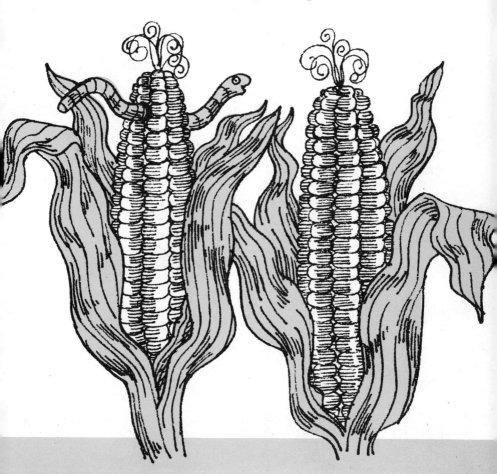

A bumblebee flying backwards
In one ear and out another
It can't knit

Why did the elephant paint
his toenails red?

How does an elephant get out
of a tree?

An elephant asked for a bed
twenty feet long and ten feet wide.
What did the salesman say?

"That's a lot of bunk!"

Waits till fall comes

They packed their trunks

To hide in a cherry tree

Mouse on a long trip

Down comes from a goose

What's the best way to get down
from an elephant?

* What is gray, has a thin tail,
   four legs, two ears, and a trunk?

Why were the elephants late
going into Noah's ark?

What's a smart duck called?

What does a duck always do
when it stands on one leg?

How many ducks are there when—
there is a duck between two ducks,
a duck behind two ducks,
and a duck in front of two ducks?

Wise quacker!   Holds up the other   Three

What did the little pig have to say
before his uncle let him up?

How is a pig's tail like getting up
at two in the morning?

What did the pig say when his side hurt?

Oh, my achin' bacon!

Both are twirly (too early)

Oinkle!

When Noah built the ark, where did he strike the first nail?

Where was Noah when night came?

What did Noah say after getting all the animals in the ark?

On the head

He was in d'ark

"Now I herd (heard) everything"

Why didn't the animals play cards in the ark?

Which animals were not in pairs?

When the animals left the ark,
Noah said, "Go forth and multiply."
Which ones disobeyed him?

Noah sat on the deck   Worms—they were in apples   Snakes—they were adders

Where did the pig get his new tail?

Where did the sheep get a haircut?

What happens when a cat eats a lemon?

Becomes a sourpuss

At a ba-ba shop

At a retail store

How can you stop a bull from charging?

What is a sleeping bull?

What's as big as the biggest bull,
but doesn't weigh an ounce?

Take away its credit card
A bulldozer
Its shadow

What did Mr. Gnu say when his wife said
  her family couldn't come to visit?

What did Mother Sardine say to
  Baby Sardine when a submarine passed?

What did Mrs. Pig tell her sad little pig
  when he was feeling blue?

"Porc-u-pine!"

"Look, a can of people"

"No Gnus is good news"

NINETY-NINE CLUMP

NINETY-NINE CLUMP

"Shall we walk or take the dog?"

Centipede with a wooden leg

Her sons had gone to the dogs

Why did Mother Flea cry?

What goes ninety-nine, clump, ninety-nine, clump?

What did Mr. Flea ask Mrs. Flea?

Alexander the Grape   Paul Onion   Moby Pickle   The Lone Tangerine   Elvis Parsley

What's purple and conquered the world?

What's large, white, and very strong?

What's green and lives in salt water?

What's orange and wears a mask?

What's green and sings?

What's worse than raining cats and dogs?

When does it rain money?

What's raised in many countries
where the rainfall is heavy?

What time of year is it when
an Indian tries to hitch a ride?

Why does an Indian chief wear
a feather headdress?

What did
the Indian boy say
when his dog
ran away?

"Dog-gone!"

To keep his wig-wam

Indian thumber

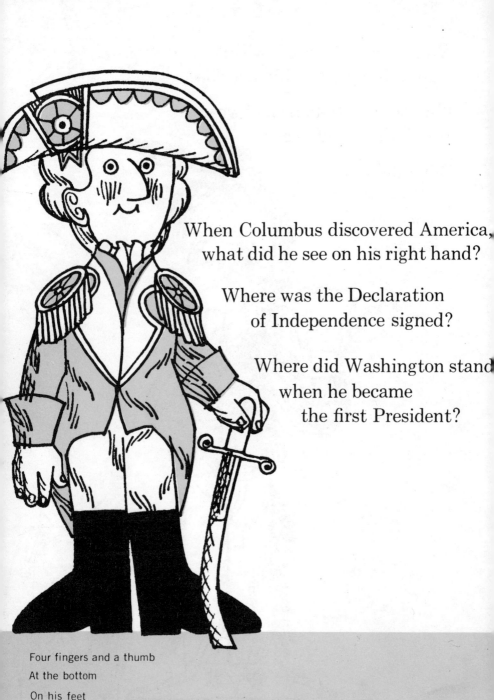

When Columbus discovered America,
what did he see on his right hand?

Where was the Declaration
of Independence signed?

Where did Washington stand
when he became
the first President?

Four fingers and a thumb
At the bottom
On his feet

How can you tell land from ocean?

How much difference is there between
the North Pole and the South Pole?

Why couldn't Silly-Willy find
the English Channel?

One's dirty, the other is tidy   A world of difference   He looked on TV

Before Australia was discovered,
   what was the smallest continent?

What is Australia bounded by?

What is found in the middle of Australia
   and also in the middle of America?

What can give you the power
to see through brick walls?

What weighs the same,
no matter how big it is?

What's round at both ends
and high in the middle?

Windows   A hole   Ohio

Meat

Moved to the back of a crowded bus

He holds up traffic

Why is Traffic Officer O'Brien so strong?

Mr. Bumble fell over forty feet but
wasn't hurt. How did this happen?

Mr. Ham, a butcher, is six feet tall,
wears a forty-six inch belt and shoes
that are size eleven. What does he weigh?

Why was the astronaut eating a sandwich
when his spaceship lifted off?

If an athlete gets athlete's foot,
what does an astronaut get?

How many redheaded men have been born
in Kansas City?

Why can't a boy walk more than
halfway into a woods?

Why does a boy put his right shoe
on first?

Where did the girl keep her dog?

What happened to the girl
who swallowed a spoon?

Which hand should a young lady
use to stir her tea?

In a barking lot
She couldn't stir
Neither, use a spoon

Why won't the boys send letters
to Washington?

How can an old lady keep stamps
from sticking together?

Washington's dead
Buy one at a time

What letters are not in the alphabet?

What begins with P, ends with E, and
   has more than a hundred letters?

Guess what remains the same
   if you take away the first letter,
   take away the last letter,
   then take away every letter?

Those in the mailbox   Post office   Postman

Why did the prisoner ask the guard
for a hammer and nail?

What about a bright pink horse?

What's dark underneath, white on top,
and hot in the summer?

What did the wall say to the wallpaper?

What did one faucet say to the other?

What did the workman say to the wall?

"You're stuck-up"   "Don't be a drip"   "One more crack, I'll plaster you"

Why are cemeteries locked at night?

What gets you into a haunted house?

Did you hear the story about the empty box?

People are dying to get in
Skeleton key
Nothing in it!